RESTORING THE PREEMINENCE OF JESUS CHRIST IN BUSINESS

The Ultimate Unfair Competitive Advantage!

LERAY HEYNE

VOLUME 1
Authentic Disciples

Windows of Heaven Inc.
PO Box 27154
Anaheim Hills, CA 92809
windowsofheaven.com

DEDICATION

I dedicate this work to my parents and wife, Teresa.

To my parents Norman and Loretta Heyne, who never ceased praying for me and sacrificed everything for me to live this calling.

To Teresa, the love of my life, who has endured more than anybody should and by the grace of God, 33 years later, is still by my side.

I love each of you more than words can express.

ENDORSEMENTS

"I am a new person in Christ because I daily offer myself as a living sacrifice. To me that's the beauty of living in communion with the Holy Spirit. Knowing my days are spent in participation with the Lord in every facet of my life and doing it for His glory brings me joy and inner peace that is unmatched. Thank you, Leray, for your guidance and wisdom in helping me live a life in communion with the Holy Spirit."

Brenda Williams
President/CEO
Artistic Printing & Specialty Advertising

"Thanks for all that you do, Leray. I appreciate how you have challenged me spiritually in so many ways. This has resulted in spiritual breakthrough for me, for my family and for the company. I would have not taken those steps without you first challenging me, but more importantly coming alongside me through the process. You are an awesome man of God and I count myself blessed to call you friend. Thank you for helping me see the miracles of God all around us in the marketplace. You are truly a blessing to me and so many others! God Bless!"

Mike Mellace
CO-Founder & CEO
Mellace Family Brands, Inc.

"Deeper still. As someone who has walked these long years with God under the influence of the Holy Spirit, I'm reminded that I've been called to a deeper walk and confident trust in all that God has made available to me in His Word. Thank-you, Leray, for your steadfastness, encouragement and patience in your ministry to me. Thank-you for being a brother in Christ Jesus as we endeavor with confidence, for all that He has in store as we go deeper still: A work in progress."

Charlie Mirarchi
Founder/CEO
Country Archer

"I've been a Christian for 20-plus years, and have never felt more alive while walking and living in the Spirit. I love the way the Spirit flows through Leray as our Lord uses him to mentor me and many others in living a life in communion with the Holy Spirit."

Michael Waitkus
President/CEO
E&E Sales Corp.

"Pastor Leray has been significantly responsible for where my current spiritual life is through showing me how to live in communion with the Holy Spirit. He took me from having the Holy Spirit just be part of my daily life as a believer to allowing Him to change the direction of the business, as well."

Keith A. Hogan
President
Private Label Partners

"Leray, I want to thank you for being my marketplace pastor and Godly brother who has helped me re-center my life. I now fit my schedule around God and do not try to shove Him into my schedule. I realize that God makes things happen, not me. Ultimately the faith you have helped me build translates into peace beyond all understanding and has made building a business more enjoyable and one that glorifies God. My relationships with family, friends and employees are stronger and deeper as a result. One will never know God's plans until he/she spends time with the Lord and you have challenged me and made me focus on doing that amid the business of life. The joy of the Lord is only found by seeking Him, which in turn, has made my whole life more fruitful and peaceful even during the storms. I am very grateful to have someone like you in my life!"

Mike Runion
Co-Founder and V.P. of Sales
Mellace Family Brands, Inc.

CONTENTS

FOREWORD i

HOW TO USE THIS BOOK
Instructions iii

PREFACE
The Prophetic Word for this Work v

THE PREEMINENCE OF JESUS CHRIST
Restoring the Preeminence of Jesus Christ in Business 2

AUTHENTIC DISCIPLES
Introduction 8
Self-Sacrificial Life 9
Abiding in the Presence of Jesus 11
Communion of the Holy Spirit 14
Mighty Acts 17
Jesus Christ Manifested 20

COMMUNION OF THE HOLY SPIRIT LIFESTYLE
Phase 1 of Holy Temple Blueprint 24
The Holy Spirit Teaches All Things 26
Life Circumstances 29
Seeking & Renewing 32
Spiritual Exercise 35
Spiritual Experiences 38
Spiritual Discernment 41
Endgame 44
The Kingdom of God 46
Transformation 48
Communion Lifestyle Diagram 50
Putting It All Together 51

THE ULTIMATE UNFAIR COMPETITIVE ADVANTAGE 56

MAKING DISCIPLES 60

A WORD TO CEOS, PRESIDENTS & OWNERS 64

THE HOLY TEMPLE OF THE SPIRIT OF GOD
Blueprint 70
Blueprint Explained 71

SEE YOU SOON! 75

FOREWORD

This devotional book needed to be written, and Leray Heyne was the man to write it. For Leray, this is not theory, this is a lifestyle. And this is not an "I-hope-it-works" book, but a tried and true, effective tool. And as you follow his lead in reading and applying Scripture to your life, you will soon become caught up in the power of God's Word and its tremendous impact in your business, your marriage and your life.

Leray Heyne's journey has taught him some valuable lessons about communicating with the Holy Spirit and of the importance of placing Jesus Christ in the proper and preeminent place in our lives and businesses. I first met Leray several years ago at a conference we were both attending. We connected and have remained friends talking frequently through the ensuing years. Leray's path has led him to the development of a powerful ministry to Christian CEO's who both need and desire to learn how to follow the Holy Spirit in the development of their business.

My experience as both a pastor and a Christian business consultant has revealed to me that our prayers are often an exercise where we do all the talking and very little listening. Obviously a wrong emphasis in this important spiritual exercise and Leray addresses this head on. In this book, Leray has added a new element to book reading as well. In fact he states it clearly at the beginning: spend less time reading and more time in communion with the Holy Spirit. This is not intended to be a quick read: rather a tool for ongoing fellowship with the Lord that we all need. I am confident that as you follow the clear outline of meditating, journaling, stating your belief, and then praying with expectancy and intimacy, you will find a closeness to the Lord and sure direction for your life and business.

The benefits of Holy Spirit-led thinking and the focus on the preeminence of Jesus Christ should not be underestimated. Leray has practiced this for years, he has instilled this in others in a life- changing way, and now offers this tremendous gift to the body of Christ at large.

Thank-you, Leray, for producing this powerful tool. And to each one who reads and follows the outline: May God add His favor to all that He calls for you to do and be for Him!

Rich Marshall

Author of the God@Work series
Founder ROI Ministry

HOW TO USE THIS BOOK

This workbook is written in a devotion-style format. It is designed so that you spend less time reading and more time in communion with the Holy Spirit, allowing Him to not only impart revelation but also transform your heart.

Instructions

Each message includes a time of meditation, space for journaling, room to make a belief statement and a place for your prayer request.

Meditate

In communion with the Holy Spirit, quiet your mind in a time of silence. As the Holy Spirit reveals things to you, ponder them with Him. In these times of meditating with the Holy Spirit, He will take you on a journey seeking out the deep things of God, imparting spiritual wisdom, knowledge and understanding. (1 Corinthians 2:10–16)

Journal

Journal and date what you saw, heard and pondered in your time of meditation. Journaling is a powerful tool in helping anchor what God the Holy Spirit is putting in your mind and writing on your heart. (Hebrews 8:10)

Belief Statement

With each message, document what you believe. In the Lifestyle portion, you will learn your belief is the first action that activates the Holy Spirit in maturing a belief into its fullness.

Prayer

"Ask anything according to Me and I will do it." (John 14:13) If it is no longer you who lives but Christ living in you (Galatians 2:20), then everything you pray for pertains to Him, and He will grant it.

If you invest the quiet time to follow this format, the Holy Spirit will bring you into a realm of profound intimacy and accelerate your transformation in the Lord.

Small Groups

Prior to each gathering, do the devotions you intend to discuss with one another. Be willing to be vulnerable and transparent as you share your personal experience with each message. As you are open with one another, you will be richly blessed as the Holy Spirit ministers through you and to you as a body.

I pray the Lord blesses your journey as you participate with the Holy Spirit to restore the preeminence of Jesus Christ in business.

PREFACE

One day in 2000 the Lord had a divine appointment scheduled for me. On that day, a friend dropped by my office unexpectedly and brought a pastor who I didn't know. In our visit together, the pastor opened his Bible and prophesied these verses over me:

"'All this,' said David, 'the Lord made me understand in writing, by His hand upon me, all the works of these plans.' And David said to his son Solomon, 'Be strong and of good courage, and do it; do not fear nor be dismayed, for the Lord God—my God—will be with you. He will not leave you nor forsake you, until you have finished all the work for the service of the house of the Lord. Here are the divisions of the priests and the Levites for all the service of the house of God; and every willing craftsman will be with you for all manner of workmanship, for every kind of service; also the leaders and all the people will be completely at your command.'"
(1 Chronicles 28:19–21, NKJV)

As he prophesied he said to me; "You're going to write a book." In my ignorance, I laughed out loud like Sarah and said, "Yeah right; that will never happen."

What you're holding in your hand is the first installment of the prophecy. Through a lifestyle in communion with the Holy Spirit, I came into agreement with the word of the Lord. I learned, like Solomon, I have been called to build a temple; not a physical one but a spiritual house, a dwelling place for the Spirit of God.

"Now, therefore, you are no longer strangers and foreigners, but fellow citizens with the saints and members of the household of God, having been built on the foundation of the apostles and prophets, Jesus Christ Himself being the chief cornerstone, in whom the whole building, being fitted together, grows into a holy temple in the Lord, in whom you also are being built together for a dwelling place of God in the Spirit."
(Ephesians 2:19–22, NKJV)

The Holy Temple of the Lord

Over the years after the prophecy, the Lord imparted to me a blueprint for building this temple. At the end of this book, I give you the architectural plan the Holy Spirit has made me understand by His hand upon me. At that time, you will learn why this volume is entirely dedicated to Phase 1 of 4 phases. You'll also understand how Phase 1 reverses the delayed state the universal Church is currently in, in becoming the Holy Temple of the Spirit of God.

I pray we, the Church, delay no further...in Jesus' name. AMEN!

Leray

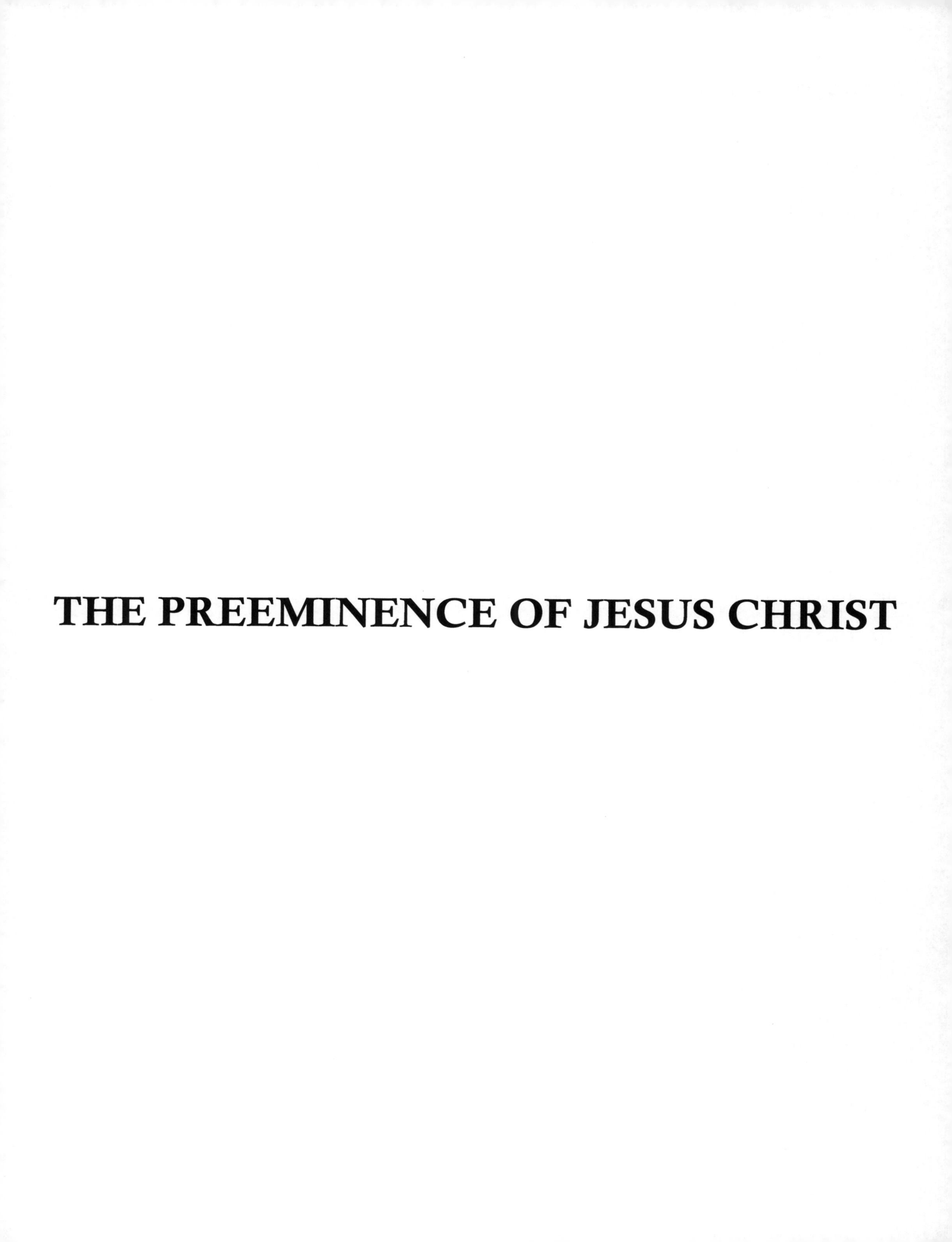

THE PREEMINENCE OF JESUS CHRIST

RESTORING THE PREEMINENCE OF JESUS CHRIST IN BUSINESS

In my 10th year of ministry, the Holy Spirit withdrew me from the CEOs I was working with, and sequestered me in His private chambers for 6 months. In this season, He gave me a greater revelation of Jesus Christ and refined in me His vision for Windows of Heaven. It was when I came out of this season, my life and ministry became all about the preeminence of Jesus Christ.

Preeminence of Christ

"He is the image of the invisible God, the firstborn over all creation. For by Him all things were created that are in heaven and that are on earth, visible and invisible, whether thrones or dominions or principalities or powers. All things were created through Him and for Him. And He is before all things, and in Him all things consist. And He is the head of the body, the church, who is the beginning, the firstborn from the dead, that in all things He may have the preeminence."
(Colossians 1:15–18, NKJV)

Jesus is the living God and His Spirit abides in His body (the Church), not on business entities. Therefore, when I make the statement, "We are restoring the preeminence of Jesus Christ in business," this means we are participating with the Holy Spirit transforming the Church into all of the fullness of Jesus Christ. (Ephesians 4:11-13) Especially those members of the Body of Christ who have been appointed to the business subculture of nations. (John 15:16, Matthew 28:19, Mark 16:15)

Preeminence is defined as: "to be first." The NIV translates preeminence as "supremacy." Supremacy means: "The state or condition of being superior to all others in authority."

The Beginning

Jesus is called "The Beginning" because He is the source of all creation. (Proverbs 8:22-31)

"In the beginning was the Word, and the Word was with God, and the Word was God."
(John 1:1, NKJV)

"'I am the Alpha and the Omega, the Beginning and the End,' says the Lord, 'who is and who was and who is to come, the Almighty.'"
(Revelation 1:8, NKJV)

Beginning is defined as: "the first." Jesus Christ is "the first" and is to be first in everything at all times. With the Church, this is exclusively true without exception. (Ephesians 1:22)

Why Business?

This is an easy one. "All things" includes every person in every nation who has employment in the business subculture of nations.

"But this is a people robbed and plundered; All of them are snared in holes, And they are hidden in prison houses; They are for prey, and no one delivers; For plunder, and no one says, 'Restore!'"
(Isaiah 42:22, NKJV)

"Also I heard the voice of the Lord, saying: 'Whom shall I send, And who will go for Us?' Then I said, 'Here am I! Send me.'"
(Isaiah 6:8, NKJV)

If you agree, please join me in making this declaration: "Lord Jesus, I declare in agreement with you: Restore! your preeminence in the business subculture of nations, as it was in the beginning. Lord, I myself will go for this cause! Send me."

Examining Ourselves *(1 Corinthians 11:28, Galatians 6:4)*
If you were to ask your secular coworkers if they see Jesus Christ being first in every aspect of your lifestyle, you might hear something like: "REALLY? Are you kidding me? Is that a trick question?"

"And He has put all things under His feet and has appointed Him the universal and supreme Head of the church [a headship exercised throughout the church]."
(Ephesians 1:22, AMP)

"He also is the Head of [His] body, the church; seeing He is the Beginning, the Firstborn from among the dead, so that He alone in everything and in every respect might occupy the chief place [stand first and be preeminent]."
(Colossians 1:18, AMP)

For most of us in the body of Christ, our coworkers' sentiments would not be unjust. A Christian business owner asking this question of a customer, vendor, employee or competitor would likely hear even a louder response, again probably not unjust for many Christian business owners.

"For the time has come for judgment to begin at the house of God; and if it begins with us first, What will be the end of those who do not obey the gospel of God?"
(1 Peter 4:17, NKJV)

Restoring the preeminence of Jesus Christ starts first with the body of Christ. Experientially I still have a long ways to go with this and I'm sure you do as well. So let's press on...together.

Date: ____________________

Meditate

Meditate on Colossians 1:15–18, allowing the Holy Spirit to impart a greater revelation and desire for the preeminence of Jesus Christ to rule and reign in you.

Journal

Journal what you saw, heard and pondered in your time of meditation.

Belief Statement

Document what you believe.

Prayer

"Ask anything according to Me and I will do it."

AUTHENTIC DISCIPLES

INTRODUCTION

Jesus has given the Church the privilege to participate with Him in restoring His preeminence in all things on earth. This requires that the Church habitually lives in covenant as authentic disciples. Most Christians are uninformed of what a post-Pentecost disciple is, so let me give you the description of an authentic disciple.

An authentic disciple is a person who habitually lives a self-sacrificial life abiding in the living person of Jesus Christ. Baptized with power, a disciple lives an experiential lifestyle in ***communion** with the Holy Spirit, manifesting mighty acts of love, faith, gifts and signs confirming their discipleship.

***Communion** is a person's participation with the presence of the Holy Spirit as He manifests the Spirit of Jesus Christ in their mortal flesh.

"The greatest hindrance in making disciples of the Church is that the churchgoing Christian already believes they are a disciple."

In this section I seek to strengthen your faith in characteristics of an authentic disciple. In the next section I will give you the how-to's for living as an authentic disciple. As you go through the messages, refer back to this description. You may even want to put it on a 3 x 5 card for reference.

SELF-SACRIFICIAL LIFE

One morning while having breakfast with a CEO, they said, "Leray, as I listened to you talk about the ministry and all the great work the Lord is doing, I keep hearing over and over in my spirit this one question: What does it cost a business owner to work with you?" I replied, "It costs a CEO their life."

"And he who does not take his cross and follow after Me is not worthy of Me. He who finds his life will lose it, and he who loses his life for My sake will find it."
(Matthew 10:38–39, NKJV)

Forsake All

"Now great multitudes went with Him. And He turned and said to them, "If anyone comes to Me and does not hate his father and mother, wife and children, brothers and sisters, yes, and his own life also, he cannot be My disciple. And whoever does not bear his cross and come after Me cannot be My disciple. For which of you, intending to build a tower, does not sit down first and count the cost, whether he has enough to finish it—lest, after he has laid the foundation, and is not able to finish, all who see it begin to mock him, saying, 'This man began to build and was not able to finish.' Or what king, going to make war against another king, does not sit down first and consider whether he is able with ten thousand to meet him who comes against him with twenty thousand? Or else, while the other is still a great way off, he sends a delegation and asks conditions of peace. So likewise, whoever of you does not forsake all that he has cannot be My disciple."
(Luke 14:25–33, NKJV)

"Those who have ears to hear, let them hear!"

Living Sacrifice

"I APPEAL to you therefore, brethren, and beg of you in view of [all] the mercies of God, to make a decisive dedication of your bodies [presenting all your members and faculties] as a living sacrifice, holy (devoted, consecrated) and well pleasing to God, which is your reasonable (rational, intelligent) service and spiritual worship."
(Romans 12:1, AMP)

This verse not only communicates that you must offer yourself daily, but more importantly, that you should offer yourself once-for-all-time unconditionally and permanently as an acceptable living sacrifice. Paul says it's reasonable for God to ask you to habitually live your life as a bondservant to Jesus Christ for His glory and unrestricted use.

Authentic discipleship has and always will cost an individual their life. The Holy Spirit didn't prompt this CEO to ask me about money, the Holy Spirit wanted to reveal to this person what the real cost was for what he was seeking.

Date: ____________________

Meditate

Self (the control of one's life) is probably the hardest and the most fearful thing to let go of. Meditate on living habitually as a living sacrifice, dead unto yourself, giving Jesus, from this day forward, unrestricted use of your life.

Journal

Journal what you saw, heard and pondered in your time of meditation.

Belief Statement

Document what you believe.

Prayer

"Ask anything according to Me and I will do it."

ABIDING IN THE PRESENCE OF JESUS

Abide

After the cross, resurrection and sending of the Holy Spirit, a disciple's relationship transitions from being an external following to an internal abiding. Authentic disciples abide in the Spirit of the living God, a spiritual union of one, the Spirit of God in them and them in the Spirit of God. (John 4:23-24, 17:20–23) An authentic disciple's reality is no longer "what would Jesus do?" but rather "what is Jesus doing?" (John 5:19)

"At that day you will know that I am in My Father, and you in Me, and I in you."
(John 14:20, NKJV)

"But you are not in the flesh but in the Spirit, if indeed the Spirit of God dwells in you. Now if anyone does not have the Spirit of Christ, he is not His."
(Romans 8:9, NKJV)

"Do you not know that you are the temple of God and that the Spirit of God dwells in you?"
(1 Corinthians 3:16, NKJV)

"And what agreement has the temple of God with idols? For you are the temple of the living God. As God has said: 'I will dwell in them And walk among them. I will be their God, And they shall be My people.'"
(2 Corinthians 6:16, NKJV)

"Therefore let that abide in you which you heard from the beginning. If what you heard from the beginning abides in you, you also will abide in the Son and in the Father."
(1 John 2:24, NKJV)

Presence

Cultivating a consciousness of presence is something I spend a lot of time on in my own life and in my one-on-ones with CEOs. Living in the reality that Jesus Christ, the living God, is present at all times and in every circumstance is a game changer for us to live as mighty disciples.

- Jesus promised never to leave you (John 14:16, 14:18)
- Jesus dwells with you NOW! (John 14:17)
- Jesus is in you NOW! (John 14:17)
- Jesus is upon you NOW! (Act 1:8)
- Jesus makes His home with you NOW! (John 14:23)

Read with new glasses, John 14 through 16. Stop to ponder some of Jesus' statements from the perspective of His presence with you now. If it helps, visualize Jesus standing right next to you in one of your current life circumstances.

The Unseen Reality

Unseen is defined as: "a belief that there is a realm controlled by a divine spirit, *syn*: spiritual world, spiritual domain." When the unseen presence of the Spirit of Jesus Christ is the reality in which you operate, you will live, speak and do as He does with humility and boldness.

Here are two examples of how authentic disciples sound when communicating to others:

- As a disciple of Jesus Christ I can do nothing of myself but what I see Jesus do; for whatever He does, I do also in like manner by the grace of the Holy Spirit in me. (John 5:19)

- I am a disciple of Jesus Christ. Do you not believe that I am in Jesus and Jesus is in me? The words that I speak to you I do not speak on my own authority; but it's Jesus who does the works you see, through the indwelling of the Holy Spirit with me. (John 14:10)

WOW! Now that's something to look forward to...Amen?

I cannot emphasize enough to get in the daily practice of cultivating the art of knowing the presence of Jesus Christ with you. Living from a conscious reality of His presence will absolutely change everything in the Church as we know it today!

Date: ____________________

Meditate

Begin spending 15 minutes, building from there, meditating on the presence of God abiding with you always.

Journal

Journal what you saw, heard and pondered in your time of meditation.

Belief Statement

Document what you believe.

Prayer

"Ask anything according to Me and I will do it."

COMMUNION OF THE HOLY SPIRIT

Shortly after the Lord made it clear that I was going to be in full-time ministry, I had this life-changing encounter with the Holy Spirit. In a time of study and prayer I looked across my office and a book caught my attention. I sensed the Holy Spirit wanted me to go over and pick it up. I noticed it was about an International business ministry we no longer hear about. As I continued in the Spirit, the Lord brought to my remembrance other large movements we no longer hear from. I became very upset, saying to the Lord, "You don't need another church, You don't need another ministry, You don't need another movement. I don't want anything to do with ministry. I am not going to be part of something that ends up coming to nothing." After a few minutes I settled down and asked the Lord this question: "Why are these ministries not growing or even existing anymore?" His answer: "Because none of them led my people into Communion with the Holy Spirit."

"The grace of the Lord Jesus Christ, and the love of God, and the communion of the Holy Spirit be with you all. Amen."
(2 Corinthians 13:14, NKJV)

Communion

Communion is translated in the Greek as "joint participation," meaning a disciple's common share in what pertains to Jesus Christ.

Dr. Kenneth Wuest was a New Testament Greek scholar. Let's look at a few of his verse translations:

Pertains to Jesus

"I have yet many things to be saying to you, but you are not able to be bearing them now so far as your understanding and receiving of them is concerned. However, whenever that One comes, the Spirit of the truth, He will lead you into all the truth, for He will not speak from himself as a source, but as many things as He hears He will speak, and the things that are coming He will make known to you. That One shall glorify me, because He shall take out from that which pertains to me and make it known to you. All things, as many as the Father has, are mine. On this account I said that He takes out from that which pertains to me and shall make it known to you."
(John 16:12–15, WUESTNT)

"Jesus is the door and communion of the Holy Spirit is the key that opens it"

Maintain a Living Communion

"I, in contradistinction to anyone else, am the vine, the genuine vine, and my Father is the tiller of the soil. Every branch in me not bearing fruit He takes away. And every branch bearing fruit, He cleanses it in order that it may keep on bearing more fruit. As for you, already you are cleansed ones because of the word which I have spoken to you. Maintain a living communion with me, and I with you. Just as the branch is unable to be bearing fruit from itself as a source unless it remains in a living union with the vine, so neither you, unless you maintain a living communion with me. As for myself, I am the vine. As for you, you are the branches. He who maintains a living communion with me and I with him, this one is bearing much fruit, because apart from me you are not able to be doing anything. If anyone is not maintaining a living communion with me, he was thrown outside as the branch is and was caused to wither. And they gather them and into the fire they throw them, and they are burned. If you maintain a living communion with me and my words

are at home in you, I command you to ask, at once, something for yourself, whatever your heart desires, and it will become yours. In this my Father is glorified, namely, that you are bearing much fruit. So shall you become my disciples."

(John 15:1–8, WUESTNT)

Joint-Participation

"Faithful is God through whom you were divinely summoned into a joint-participation with His Son, Jesus Christ our Lord."

(1 Corinthians 1:9, WUESTNT)

As we learned in the Abiding lesson, the disciple relationship transitions from being one in the flesh to being one in union with the Spirit of Jesus Christ. So it is natural to conclude that by joining these two lessons together, it is impossible to live as an authentic disciple of Jesus Christ apart from habitually living a lifestyle in communion with the Holy Spirit.

You're probably thinking, "Okay then, how do I do that?" Because this is an absolute, most of this volume is dedicated to equipping you to do just that.

The other day a brother in the Lord told me, "I can't wait for Jesus to come." I replied, "Brother I am having so much fun with Jesus right now, I hope He waits so I can finish the assignment He's given me!" Every Christian is looking forward to being with Jesus in eternity, but many are missing the fact that they can have the most amazing life with Him right now.

Date: ____________________

Meditate

Meditate on participating in your sphere of influence, with the abiding presence of Jesus.

Journal

Journal what you saw, heard and pondered in your time of meditation.

Belief Statement

Document what you believe.

Prayer

"Ask anything according to Me and I will do it."

MIGHTY ACTS

One afternoon the Lord sent me to the hospital to pray for a man who was going to have a heart procedure the next day. Many of his health issues were self-inflicted, so the Lord also gave me a stern message of correction. (1 Peter 4:11) As we prayed together the man asked the Lord for a sign confirming the message was from Him. In less than five minutes a nurse came in with two very large pink pills and said, "The doctor just called and told me to give you these and send you home." I looked at the man and said, "There's your sign!" He agreed and praised the Lord.

"Most assuredly, I say to you, he who believes in Me, the works that I do he will do also; and greater works than these he will do, because I go to My Father."
(John 14:12, NKJV)

"But you shall receive power (ability, efficiency, and might) when the Holy Spirit has come upon you, and you shall be My witnesses in Jerusalem and all Judea and Samaria and to the ends (the very bounds) of the earth."
(Acts 1:8, AMP)

Mighty God

One of the names of Jesus is: "Mighty God." (Isaiah 9:6) When the Spirit of God enters the human soul He does not void any of His authority or attributes as Mighty God. In fact authentic disciples are also known as mighty disciples.

"In mighty signs and wonders, by the power of the Spirit of God, so that from Jerusalem and round about to Illyricum I have fully preached the gospel of Christ."
(Romans 15:19, NKJV)

"Truly the signs of an apostle were accomplished among you with all perseverance, in signs and wonders and mighty deeds."
(2 Corinthians 12:12, NKJV)

"Since you seek a proof of Christ speaking in me, who is not weak toward you, but mighty in you."
(2 Corinthians 13:3, NKJV)

"And what is the exceeding greatness of His power toward us who believe, according to the working of His mighty power"
(Ephesians 1:19, NKJV)

Confirming Discipleship

When the Holy Spirit confirms a disciple's word with accompanying signs, He's also confirming the authenticity of a disciple's partnership with His living presence.

"And these signs will accompany those who believe: in my name they will cast out demons; they will speak in new tongues; they will pick up serpents with their hands; and if they drink any deadly poison, it will not hurt them; they will lay their hands on the sick, and they will recover."
(Mark 16:17–18, ESV)

"So then the Lord Jesus, after he had spoken to them, was taken up into heaven and sat down at the right hand of God. And they went out and preached everywhere, while the Lord worked with them and confirmed the message by accompanying signs."
(Mark 16:19–20, ESV)

Beyond Imagination

"Now to Him who is able to do exceedingly abundantly above all that we ask or think, according to the power that works in us."
(Ephesians 3:20, NKJV)

Did you catch that? You have an opportunity by the power that works "in you" to participate with supernatural acts that are so far beyond anything you can imagine, ask or think!

Date: ____________________

Meditate

We all need a greater reality of the infinite power of Jesus Christ that abides in us. In your time of meditation, let the Holy Spirit reveal and purge areas of unbelief. Then start exercising bold acts of faith, believing the Lord to confirm them with accompanying signs.

Journal

Journal what you saw, heard and pondered in your time of meditation.

Belief Statement

Document what you believe.

Prayer

"Ask anything according to Me and I will do it."

JESUS CHRIST MANIFESTED

We have reached the last message of this section. Before we move on to the lifestyle section, let's look at the way the presence of Jesus Christ is tangibly manifested in the mortal body of an authentic disciple.

"I have been crucified with Christ; it is no longer I who live, but Christ lives in me; and the life which I now live in the flesh I live by faith in the Son of God, who loved me and gave Himself for me."
(Galatians 2:20, NKJV)

Manifest

One of the functions of the Holy Spirit is to reveal Jesus Christ to the world. (John 15:26, 16:14, Acts 1:8) As temples of the Holy Spirit, authentic disciples receive authority to participate with the Holy Spirit as He manifests the Spirit of Jesus Christ in their mortal bodies. (1Corinthians 6:19-20)

"For I know that this will turn out for my deliverance through your prayer and the supply of the Spirit of Jesus Christ, according to my earnest expectation and hope that in nothing I shall be ashamed, but with all boldness, as always, so now also Christ will be magnified in my body, whether by life or by death."
(Philippians 1:19–20, NKJV)

"But we have this treasure in earthen vessels, that the excellence of the power may be of God and not of us. We are hard-pressed on every side, yet not crushed; we are perplexed, but not in despair; persecuted, but not forsaken; struck down, but not destroyed—always carrying about in the body the dying of the Lord Jesus, that the life of Jesus also may be manifested in our body. For we who live are always delivered to death for Jesus' sake, that the life of Jesus also may be manifested in our mortal flesh."
(2 Corinthians 4:7–11, NKJV)

Manifest is defined as: "to make clear or obvious to the eye or mind."

Authentic disciples live self-sacrificial lives dead unto themselves, so it is no longer they who live but Christ living in them. In this manner Jesus becomes preeminent (the first), the authentic disciple becomes second, partnering with the indwelling life of Christ through a lifestyle of communion with the Holy Spirit.

It's in this way authentic disciples make clear to the world how the preeminence of Jesus Christ is to rule and reign in a person's life.

Date: ____________________

Meditate
As you meditate on these scriptures, ask what will it take for more of the fullness of Jesus Christ to tangibly manifest in your mortal body.

Journal
Journal what you saw, heard and pondered in your time of meditation.

Belief Statement
Document what you believe.

Prayer
"Ask anything according to Me and I will do it."

COMMUNION OF THE HOLY SPIRIT LIFESTYLE

PHASE 1 OF THE HOLY TEMPLE BLUEPRINT

Visual aids can help in understanding a subject, so before we explore aspects of the lifestyle, let's look at Phase 1 of the Holy Temple Blueprint. It summarizes how to live as an authentic disciple in communion with the Holy Spirit.

Our new birth in Christ makes us partakers of the spiritual life; A life that in the beginning is foreign to us. To know it fully we need to acquire a new lifestyle. This new way is known as living and walking in communion with the Holy Spirit. (Galatians 5:25)

I am going to be up front in telling you that acquiring this new lifestyle will require your absolute discipline. Living in a new way is not something you can just pray to take place without active participation in the change.

Be encouraged to know as you live in communion with the Holy Spirit, there will be a time when your experiences with the Spirit of God transform you to live from His love. To see this for yourself look at the top of the diagram. One of the first steps on your journey as an authentic disciple is to love the Lord with all your heart, soul and mind. (Matthew 22:36-38) Disciples who patiently stay engaged in the communion lifestyle have their discipline swallowed up by LOVE, which becomes the new force from which they live.

As you can see, Jesus is restoring His disciples to live a life in the Spirit, **by** the power of the Holy Spirit, **from** the abiding love of the Spirit of God.

Okay, let's proceed. I recommend referring back to this diagram as you go through the messages.

PHASE 1

"You shall **love** your God with all your heart, with all your soul and with all your mind."

LOVE

Faith experienced in Communion with the Holy Spirit grows love for the Lord

EXPERIENCED

Wisdom exercised in Communion with the Holy Spirit manifest faith

EXERCISED

Seeking / Renewing practice in Communion with the Holy Spirit reveals wisdom

PRACTICED

Life & Circumstances

THE HOLY SPIRIT TEACHES ALL THINGS

Living in communion with the Holy Spirit requires an absolute belief that the Father and Jesus sent the Holy Spirit to teach and guide you in all things as an authentic disciple. (John 14:16, 15:26) It may take some time for your senses to discern and know the Holy Spirit's presence, but be assured if you believe and desire to know Him, He will make Himself known to you.

"Ask, and it will be given to you; seek, and you will find; knock, and it will be opened to you. For everyone who asks receives, and he who seeks finds, and to him who knocks it will be opened."
(Matthew 7:7–8, NKJV)

In my first three years at church I never received any teaching about the Holy Spirit. Because of circumstances in my life, I became desperate to know the Holy Spirit. So for as long as I can remember, I started every morning opening my Bible to John 14:26 and recited this to the Lord: "You said, the Holy Spirit would teach me all things. I am here. Have the Holy Spirit teach me."

"But the Helper, the Holy Spirit, whom the Father will send in My name, He will teach you all things, and bring to your remembrance all things that I said to you."
(John 14:26, NKJV)

"But the anointing which you have received from Him abides in you, and you do not need that anyone teach you; but as the same anointing teaches you concerning all things, and is true, and is not a lie, and just as it has taught you, you will abide in Him."
(1 John 2:27, NKJV)

As you read this, I hope it strengthens your faith to see how my life has become a living testimony of this truth. I am praying for it to become yours too. Believe!

"And he believed in the Lord, and He accounted it to him for righteousness."
(Genesis 15:6, NKJV)

Agreement

Living in agreement with the Holy Spirit is another stipulation of living in communion with Him (agreement: one accord in mind, purpose and action).

"But God has revealed them to us through His Spirit. For the Spirit searches all things, yes, the deep things of God. For what man knows the things of a man except the spirit of the man which is in him? Even so no one knows the things of God except the Spirit of God. Now we have received, not the spirit of the world, but the Spirit who is from God, that we might know the things that have been freely given to us by God. These things we also speak, not in words which man's wisdom teaches but which the Holy Spirit teaches, comparing spiritual things with spiritual. But the natural man does not receive the things of the Spirit of God, for they are foolishness to him; nor can he know them, because they are spiritually discerned. But he who is spiritual judges all things, yet he himself is rightly judged by no one. For 'who has known the mind of the Lord that he may instruct Him?' But we have the mind of Christ."
(1 Corinthians 2:10–16, NKJV)

Having the mind of Christ is a prerequisite for a disciple to participate in the life of Christ. To obtain the mind of Christ a disciple must live in agreement with the Holy Spirit. (John 15:14-15; 16:13)

Date: ____________________

Meditate

The Holy Spirit will teach and guide you in all things. Meditate on believing and living in agreement with this truth.

Journal

Journal what you saw, heard and pondered in your time of meditation.

Belief Statement

Document what you believe.

Prayer

"Ask anything according to Me and I will do it."

LIFE CIRCUMSTANCES

Life circumstances are where the lifestyle in communion with the Holy Spirit begins. Jesus uses a disciple's day-to-day circumstances in four ways to transform them into a mighty disciple.

- **The Holy Spirit uses life circumstances to separate a disciple from the carnal and world structures they formally operated in.**

"They are not of the world, just as I am not of the world."
(John 17:16, NKJV)

"And what agreement has the temple of God with idols? For you are the temple of the living God. As God has said: 'I will dwell in them And walk among them. I will be their God, And they shall be My people.' Therefore 'Come out from among them And be separate, says the Lord. Do not touch what is unclean, And I will receive you.' 'I will be a Father to you, And you shall be My sons and daughters, Says the Lord Almighty.'"
(2 Corinthians 6:16–18, NKJV)

"And you He made alive, who were dead in trespasses and sins, in which you once walked according to the course of this world, according to the prince of the power of the air, the spirit who now works in the sons of disobedience, among whom also we all once conducted ourselves in the lusts of our flesh, fulfilling the desires of the flesh and of the mind, and were by nature children of wrath, just as the others."
(Ephesians 2:1–3, NKJV)

- **The Holy Spirit uses life circumstances to reveal the wisdom of the Spirit of God, the knowledge of the Spirit of God, and the understanding of the Spirit of God.**

"And I have filled him with the Spirit of God, in wisdom, in understanding, in knowledge, and in all manner of workmanship."
(Exodus 31:3, NKJV)

"The Spirit of the Lord shall rest upon Him, The Spirit of wisdom and understanding, The Spirit of counsel and might, The Spirit of knowledge and of the fear of the Lord."
(Isaiah 11:2, NKJV)

"Therefore I also, after I heard of your faith in the Lord Jesus and your love for all the saints, do not cease to give thanks for you, making mention of you in my prayers: that the God of our Lord Jesus Christ, the Father of glory, may give to you the spirit of wisdom and revelation in the knowledge of Him, the eyes of your understanding being enlightened; that you may know what is the hope of His calling, what are the riches of the glory of His inheritance in the saints."
(Ephesians 1:15–18, NKJV)

"And so, from the day we heard, we have not ceased to pray for you, asking that you may be filled with the knowledge of his will in all spiritual wisdom and understanding."
(Colossians 1:9, ESV)

- **The Holy Spirit uses life circumstances to exercise a disciple's spiritual faculties and faith.**

"Jesus said to her, 'Did I not say to you that if you would believe you would see the glory of God?'"
(John 11:40, NKJV)

"Immediately the father of the child cried out and said with tears, 'Lord, I believe; help my unbelief!'"
(Mark 9:24, NKJV)

"He did not waver at the promise of God through unbelief, but was strengthened in faith, giving glory to God."
(Romans 4:20, NKJV)

- **The Holy Spirit uses life circumstances as divine encounters, drawing a disciple into experiences with His presence.**

"And when he came to the den, he cried out with a lamenting voice to Daniel. The king spoke, saying to Daniel, 'Daniel, servant of the living God, has your God, whom you serve continually, been able to deliver you from the lions?' Then Daniel said to the king, 'O king, live forever! My God sent His angel and shut the lions' mouths, so that they have not hurt me, because I was found innocent before Him; and also, O king, I have done no wrong before you.' Now the king was exceedingly glad for him, and commanded that they should take Daniel up out of the den. So Daniel was taken up out of the den, and no injury whatever was found on him, because he believed in his God."
(Daniel 6:20–23, NKJV)

"But a certain man named Ananias, with Sapphira his wife, sold a possession. And he kept back part of the proceeds, his wife also being aware of it, and brought a certain part and laid it at the apostles' feet. But Peter said, 'Ananias, why has Satan filled your heart to lie to the Holy Spirit and keep back part of the price of the land for yourself? While it remained, was it not your own? And after it was sold, was it not in your own control? Why have you conceived this thing in your heart? You have not lied to men but to God.' Then Ananias, hearing these words, fell down and breathed his last. So great fear came upon all those who heard these things."
(Acts 5:1–5, NKJV)

I believe business is an accelerated transformative course. Why? Because regardless of the job you hold in business, you are likely hit with multiple circumstances everyday that tempt you to operate in the flesh and from a world view, rather than in communion with the Holy Spirit.

So please remember, whatever life circumstance Jesus has you in, there is some level of all four of these aspects happening simultaneously. Why is this important to know? Because when you get into spiritual discernment, this knowledge will help you better discern the guiding of the Holy Spirit in the heat of circumstances.

"The greatest mystery in the Church, is how the Lord uses the things of this world, to transform them into someone who is not of this world"

Date: ____________________

Meditate
Meditate on these four ways the Lord is always active in your life as an authentic disciple.

Journal
Journal what you saw, heard and pondered in your time of meditation.

____

____

____

____

____

____

____

____

Belief Statement
Document what you believe.

____

____

____

____

Prayer
"Ask anything according to Me and I will do it."

____

____

____

____

SEEKING & RENEWING

It's very common for Christians to start their day with a daily devotion book. As an authentic disciple, your life becomes the daily devotion the Lord wants to speak to you about.

"Clearly you are an epistle of Christ, ministered by us, written not with ink but by the Spirit of the living God, not on tablets of stone but on tablets of flesh, that is, of the heart."
(2 Corinthians 3:3, NKJV)

Remember your life is one of participation with the Holy Spirit. Jesus knows you better than you know yourself. He knows where you need to be corrected, instructed, encouraged and strengthened so you can participate with Him.

"For 'who has known the mind of the Lord that he may instruct Him?' But we have the mind of Christ."
(1 Corinthians 2:16, NKJV)

"All Scripture is given by inspiration of God, and is profitable for doctrine, for reproof, for correction, for instruction in righteousness, that the man of God may be complete, thoroughly equipped for every good work."
(2 Timothy 3:16–17, NKJV)

If the Lord hasn't already revealed somethings to me, this is how I start my day: "Lord you know me better than I know myself. My life is yours. What is it that you want to speak to me about?" Then I wait on Him to speak or lead me.

Seeking and Renewing serve two different roles in the life of a disciple. In both roles the Holy Spirit uses the following in a disciple's private time to immerse them in revelation and to renew their mind:

- A disciple spends private time abiding in the Word
- A disciple spends private time praying
- A disciple spends private time worshiping
- A disciple spends private time meditating

Every Seeking and Renewing time is different. Remember the Holy Spirit is leading the private time. One day the Lord may have me intercede for people for an hour. Another He may have me study the Word for two days and then pray and meditate on it for another, all so I can come into agreement with what He's doing in a disciple's life. The point is, authentic disciples in communion with the Holy Spirit spend private time everyday seeking and renewing themselves in the life of Jesus Christ.

"My voice You shall hear in the morning, O Lord; In the morning I will direct it to You, And I will look up."
(Psalm 5:3, NKJV)

Seeking

As I shared previously, the Holy Spirit uses life circumstances to perfect disciples in the fullness of Jesus Christ. One day a CEO told me how he had reacted very pridefully and arrogantly in a circumstance. He discerned accurately that the Holy Spirit was revealing pride and arrogance, then spent the next week seeking the Lord in those areas.

- As it relates to a disciple's personal life, seeking typically happens in the process of a subject the Holy Spirit is addressing in their lifestyle.

"So I say to you, ask, and it will be given to you; seek, and you will find; knock, and it will be opened to you."
(Luke 11:9, NKJV)

Renewing

On another day, a CEO told me how the Lord was testing her faith. Notice what I said, she already had faith for the circumstance but the Lord was testing it.

- As it relates to a disciple's personal life, renewing yourself daily in your already-attained faith empowers you to persevere and live mightily in all life circumstances.

"and be renewed in the spirit of your mind."
(Ephesians 4:23, NKJV)

Meditation

In today's society most Christians are so busy they set aside very little or no time for Seeking and Renewing. Therefore, they miss out on a very important aspect of our private time with the Lord, and that is meditation. There are realms and depths of spiritual wisdom that can only be attained through meditating privately in communion with the Holy Spirit.

"But God has revealed them to us through His Spirit. For the Spirit searches all things, yes, the deep things of God."
(1 Corinthians 2:10, NKJV)

Read Psalms 119:97-104 and notice how meditation made David wiser than his enemies, wiser than his teachers and gave him more understanding than those who were much older than him.

Date: ____________________

Meditate

Meditate on Psalms 119:97-104. From this day forward, try to put aside enough time every day to meditate in your private time of Seeking and Renewing with the Lord. (Get wisdom! Proverbs 4:5,7)

Journal

Journal what you saw, heard and pondered in your time of meditation.

____

____

____

____

____

____

____

____

Belief Statement

Document what you believe.

____

____

____

____

Prayer

"Ask anything according to Me and I will do it."

____

____

____

____

SPIRITUAL EXERCISE

I am one of those people who likes to go to the gym and exercise. This is probably why I enjoy how the Holy Spirit uses life circumstances to exercise a disciple's spiritual faculties (faith and gifts).

Faith comes from hearing the word (Romans 10:17), but yet it's dead apart from faith works. (James 2:14-26)

"For as the body without the spirit is dead, so faith without works is dead also."
(James 2:26, NKJV)

Spiritual Exercise

"But solid food belongs to those who are of full age, that is, those who by reason of use have their senses exercised to discern both good and evil."
(Hebrews 5:14, NKJV)

In this passage the writer tells us that disciples who have grown to full age can handle solid food and can do so because they exercise their senses. Only through repeated exercise can a disciple's spiritual faculties mature to discern the difference between the spiritual realms of good and evil.

Here are a few examples of faith works:

- Exercise is unwavering belief
- Exercise is taking faith risks
- Exercise is using spiritual gifts
- Exercise is trusting spiritual discernment
- Exercise is enduring circumstances

Endurance

Repeated exercise that tests the physical body's limits increases strength and endurance. This is the same with a disciple's spiritual body.

"Consider it wholly joyful, my brethren, whenever you are enveloped in or encounter trials of any sort or fall into various temptations. Be assured and understand that the trial and proving of your faith bring out endurance and steadfastness and patience. But let endurance and steadfastness and patience have full play and do a thorough work, so that you may be [people] perfectly and fully developed [with no defects], lacking in nothing."
(James 1:2–4, AMP)

Precious Stones

The Lord calls you a precious, living stone. Have you ever considered how precious stones are made?

"Come to Him [then, to that] Living Stone which men tried and threw away, but which is chosen [and] precious in God's sight. [Come] and, like living stones, be yourselves built [into] a spiritual house, for a holy (dedicated, consecrated) priesthood, to offer up [those] spiritual sacrifices [that are] acceptable and pleasing to God through Jesus Christ."
(1 Peter 2:4–5, AMP)

Precious stones are made by going through treatments of cutting, polishing, heat, radiation, waxing, and fracture filling. It's these types of applied pressures that make stones precious.

You are the Lord's precious, living stone. The intensity and length of a life circumstance is simply an exercise opportunity for your faith and gifts to be perfected as a mighty disciple of Jesus Christ.

Date: ____________________

Meditate

Meditate on the Word being living and powerful and not returning void. On having faith as a mustard seed so you can participate in the demonstration with the Spirit of God in power. (Hebrews 4:12, Isaiah 55:11, Matthew 17:20, 1 Corinthians 2:4)

Journal

Journal what you saw, heard and pondered in your time of meditation.

Belief Statement

Document what you believe.

Prayer

"Ask anything according to Me and I will do it."

SPIRITUAL EXPERIENCES

I previously mentioned that when we first start to live in the Spirit it is foreign to us. Spiritual experiences change all of that. Spiritual experiences are climaxes in acquiring wisdom and understanding of the Spirit of God. They are meant to be finals that transform (shift) a disciple to live in the reality of the supernatural.

Get Wisdom, Get Understanding

"Get skillful and godly Wisdom, get understanding (discernment, comprehension, and interpretation); do not forget and do not turn back from the words of my mouth. Forsake not [Wisdom], and she will keep, defend, and protect you; love her, and she will guard you. The beginning of Wisdom is: get Wisdom (skillful and godly Wisdom)! [For skillful and godly Wisdom is the principal thing.] And with all you have gotten, get understanding (discernment, comprehension, and interpretation). Prize Wisdom highly and exalt her, and she will exalt and promote you; she will bring you to honor when you embrace her. She shall give to your head a wreath of gracefulness; a crown of beauty and glory will she deliver to you."

(Proverbs 4:5–9, AMP)

Experience is defined as increased understanding (discernment, comprehension, and interpretation). So what does this mean? It means you can only acquire the fullness of divine wisdom and understanding through experiencing them in communion with the Holy Spirit.

Experiences Surpasses Knowledge

"... that the Christ might finally settle down and feel completely at home in your hearts through your faith; in love having been firmly rooted and grounded in order that you may be able to grasp with all the saints what is the breadth and width and height and depth, and to know experientially the love of the Christ which surpasses experiential knowledge in order that you may be filled up to the measure of all the fulness of God."

(Ephesians 3:13–19, WUESTNT)

Experiencing the love of Christ in participation with the Holy Spirit surpasses a disciple's experiential knowledge of Him alone.

"Living in communion with the Holy Spirit matures a disciple from the milk of the Word to the meat of the Word, not in a theological manner but in an experiential one!"

Miracles, Signs and Wonders

I observe Christians having spiritual experiences, also known as miracles, signs and wonders, every month but I am sad to see very little shift in their lifestyles. I think this is because most Christians do not live in a conscious reality that Jesus is present with them. Here's an example of what I mean. Every week I get calls from multiple people who need prayer and encouragement for business or personal finances. Shortly afterwards those same people tell me about the amazing way God provided. Then when the following month comes around and finances are tough again, the cycle repeats itself all over. Faith for finances can be one of those tests that repeats itself month after month, year after year until our belief in God's provision becomes our reality. This was the case in my life, until I made this declaration.

"Lord, forgive me if I ever ask you for faith for finances again. I don't need another miracle or sign. (John 4:48) Thank you, Lord, for showing me time and again that you know my needs before I even ask and you provide for them always as you have promised in your Word." (Matthew 6:32-34)

You may be surprised to know this declaration did not make my finance troubles go away; in fact they became worse. What changed was me. As I started living by faith, the Lord intensified my life circumstance and over time, gave me great faith for finances.

Date: ____________________

Meditate
You are in this world but not of this world. Meditate on becoming conscious of every aspect of your life as being a spiritual experience, meant to increase your faith to live a supernatural lifestyle in communion with the Holy Spirit.

Journal
Journal what you saw, heard and pondered in your time of meditation.

Belief Statement
Document what you believe.

Prayer
"Ask anything according to Me and I will do it."

SPIRITUAL DISCERNMENT

In one of my meetings with a CEO, she became so frustrated with me she blurted out, "I don't hear the voice of God like you." I replied, "You are hearing better than you think you are." On the drive back to my office, I asked the Lord to show me how to teach her, that she was hearing His voice.

The first thing the Lord had me do was to write down the different ways I have discerned His voice through experience. Here's a small portion of that list:

Sharp pain in my heart
Stomach convulsion
Heart burning
Vision (no word or thoughts)
Revealing (uncovering something)

I picked these few examples because I learned something in writing my list. With this list in front of me, I became conscious of all the different ways I had learned to discern the Lord's communications. I also realized that maybe we are doing each other an injustice by using the terms "heard" or "said." Yes, the Holy Spirits speaks (Mark 13:11, Acts 13:2) but there are so many other ways He communicates with us.

When I got back together with the CEO, I shared my list and how I had used my discernment as it related to business circumstances we had walked through together. The lightbulb came on for her, as she realized she was discerning the communications of the Lord much better then she gave herself credit for. In that meeting the Spirit of the Lord brought a release. To say this person was never the same would be a gross understatement!

"Now the Lord is the Spirit, and where the Spirit of the Lord is, there is freedom."
(2 Corinthians 3:17, ESV)

Trial-and-Error

The great apostle Paul learned spiritual discernment through trial and error. As an authentic disciple, you will also learn it in the same way.

"Then they passed through Phrygia and the Galatian region, having been forbidden by the Holy Spirit to speak the Word in Asia. And having come down to the borders of Mysia, by a trial-and-error method they kept on attempting to discover whether it was right to go to Bithynia. But the Spirit of Jesus did not permit them to do so. And having skirted Mysia they came down to Troas."
(Acts 16:6–8, WUESTNT)

Proficiency

How do you become proficient in spiritual discernment? You may not be aware of it, but I've already given you the process. You only become proficient in spiritual discernment by living a lifestyle of seeking, exercising and experiencing in communion with the Holy Spirit. Fully embrace this lifestyle and you will become proficient in the many forms of spiritual discernment.

Faith

It is impossible to please the Lord if you do not live by faith.

"But without faith it is impossible to please Him, for he who comes to God must believe that He is, and that He is a rewarder of those who diligently seek Him."
(Hebrews 11:6, NKJV)

By experience (trial and error), I have learned that a sharp pain in my heart means something is not right with the Lord. For example, if I say something that I should not have said, I may get a sharp pain in my heart letting me know the Lord was not pleased. Or if I hear something said by another and I get a sharp pain in my heart, I know the Holy Spirit doesn't agree with what was just said.

Once you believe a form of communication means something, and the Lord knows you know that's what it means, you are now responsible for living by faith with that discernment gift.

Date: ____________________

Meditate

Meditate on living a lifestyle completely led by your spiritual discernment of the Holy Spirit's communications.

Journal

Journal what you saw, heard and pondered in your time of meditation.

Belief Statement

Document what you believe.

Prayer

"Ask anything according to Me and I will do it."

ENDGAME

In your Christian walk, the term endgame is probably something you never heard before. That was the case with me until one afternoon when I was studying this subject, the Lord said to me, "You need to know what the endgame is." I pondered that for a moment and said, "Yes Lord, I need to know what the endgame is. What is it?"

"I do not pray for these alone, but also for those who will believe in Me through their word; that they all may be one, as You, Father, are in Me, and I in You; that they also may be one in Us, that the world may believe that You sent Me. And the glory which You gave Me I have given them, that they may be one just as We are one: I in them, and You in Me; that they may be made perfect in one, and that the world may know that You have sent Me, and have loved them as You have loved Me."
(John 17:20–23, NKJV)

The endgame is to be joined and made perfect in the spiritual union as one with the Father, Son and Holy Spirit so the world will see through the disciple's lifestyle that the Father sent the Son and loves those in the world as He loves His Son. The Holy Spirit has every aspect of a disciple's lifestyle individually and corporately targeted towards this one goal.

"It's never about the business, it's never about the money and it's never about the ministry!"

My mom, the founder of our company, was always conscious of the Lord's presence with us in business. For 18 years we had miracles take place every month (spiritual experiences). I can still hear her say as she walked the halls of our company, "It's never about the business!" When a Christian starts living as an authentic disciple, they quickly learn it's never about the business, it's never about the money and it's never about the ministry.

Date: ____________________

Meditate

Meditate on becoming perfected in the spiritual union as one with the Father, Son and Holy Spirit.

Journal

Journal what you saw, heard and pondered in your time of meditation.

Belief Statement

Document what you believe.

Prayer

"Ask anything according to Me and I will do it."

THE KINGDOM OF GOD

Jesus made statements such as: "What is the kingdom of God like? To what shall I liken the kingdom of God?" (Luke 13:18, 20) I don't know about you, but there was a time in my life when Jesus' parables confused me even more as to what is the kingdom of God. I still had questions like:

- Lord, if I am to first seek the kingdom of God and I find it, how will I know I have found it if I don't know what it is? (Matthew 6:33)
- Lord, if the kingdom of God abides within me, I need to know what is in me. (Luke 17:21)
- Lord, when I pray for someone who is sick and they are healed, and I tell them the kingdom of God has drawn near to them. If they ask what the kingdom of God is, what will I say if I don't know myself? (Luke 10:9)
- Lord, when I pray for the kingdom of God to come to earth as it is in heaven and it arrives, how will I recognize it if I don't know what it is? (Matthew 6:10)

It was questions like these that compelled me to seek the Lord for over 5 years to know what is the kingdom of God. Over those years I created and refined this statement so I would have something to meditate on every day.

The Kingdom of God on earth as it is in heaven is the love of the Father manifested by the Son, Jesus Christ, through the royal and divine power of His Spirit and Word reigning in glory, honor and dominion in ALL creation.

Simplified: *The manifestation of the fullness of Jesus Christ.*

I don't believe there are enough books that could ever be written to adequately define what the kingdom of God is, so I am certainly not trying to accomplish this in one statement. This definition has simply functioned for me and those who have been equipped through Windows of Heaven as a target we have our lives aimed at.

I pray this kingdom description gives you a better understanding of what the Holy Spirit wants you to participate in. When the Holy Spirit manifests the kingdom of God in you, you will participate with Him in transforming spheres of your influence to match that which is in Heaven. Praise the Lord!

Date: ____________________

Meditate

Meditate on the kingdom description every day until it becomes alive in you.

Journal

Journal what you saw, heard and pondered in your time of meditation.

Belief Statement

Document what you believe.

Prayer

"Ask anything according to Me and I will do it."

TRANSFORMATION

In Christian communities it's popular to say that we will not achieve perfection until the coming of Jesus Christ. This is true, but remember the endgame. Jesus says in John 17, there must be a degree of perfection attained in Him in order for the world to see the love of God. If the Church does not attain a degree of perfection in the fullness of Christ now, the world will never see the love He has for them.

Transformation

Transformation is defined as dramatic change in form, appearance or character. In this message I will deal with transformation in two areas, the first is with you individually and the second is with your immediate spheres of influence.

Individually

"But we all, with unveiled face, beholding as in a mirror the glory of the Lord, are being transformed into the same image from glory to glory, just as by the Spirit of the Lord."
(2 Corinthians 3:18, NKJV)

A mirror is a reflective device that accurately represents something. A disciple's life can not reflect any more of the fullness of Jesus than what they have already attained. (Ephesians 4:13)

"Not that I have already attained, or am already perfected; but I press on, that I may lay hold of that for which Christ Jesus has also laid hold of me."
(Philippians 3:12, NKJV)

John the Baptist said, "He must increase, but I must decrease." Let this be your hearts desire so the Spirit of Christ is perpetually increased and reflected in your mortal body. (John 3:30, 2 Corinthians 4:7-11, Galatians 2:20)

Spheres of Influence

Most Christians are fairly diligent in pursuing to be Christ-like, but much of their effort stops at an inward focus so unintentionally it becomes all about them. As a result, their spheres of influence never have an encounter with Jesus Christ. As I write this I recall the Samaritan woman at the well. Her encounter with Jesus not only transformed her but almost her entire city. (John 4:5-42) If we are living dead unto ourselves and it's the life of Christ living in us, every person in our spheres of influence should be having an encounter with Jesus Christ.

Attaining To

I shepherd CEOs who are typically achievers and when they are not achieving a desired result, they get down on themselves quite hard. I encourage them that I believe the Lord is pleased with a person who stays habitually engaged in the disciple lifestyle. This is the perfection I ask them to shoot for and then trust the Holy Spirit will do His transforming part.

"So he answered and said to me: 'This is the word of the Lord to Zerubbabel: "Not by might nor by power, but by My Spirit," Says the Lord of hosts.'"
(Zechariah 4:6, NKJV)

Date: ____________________

Meditate
Meditate on letting the transforming power of the Holy Spirit live in you.. and through you...more! "Do not quench the Spirit." (1 Thessalonians 5:19, NKJV)

Journal
Journal what you saw, heard and pondered in your time of meditation.

Belief Statement
Document what you believe.

Prayer
"Ask anything according to Me and I will do it."

COMMUNION LIFESTYLE DIAGRAM

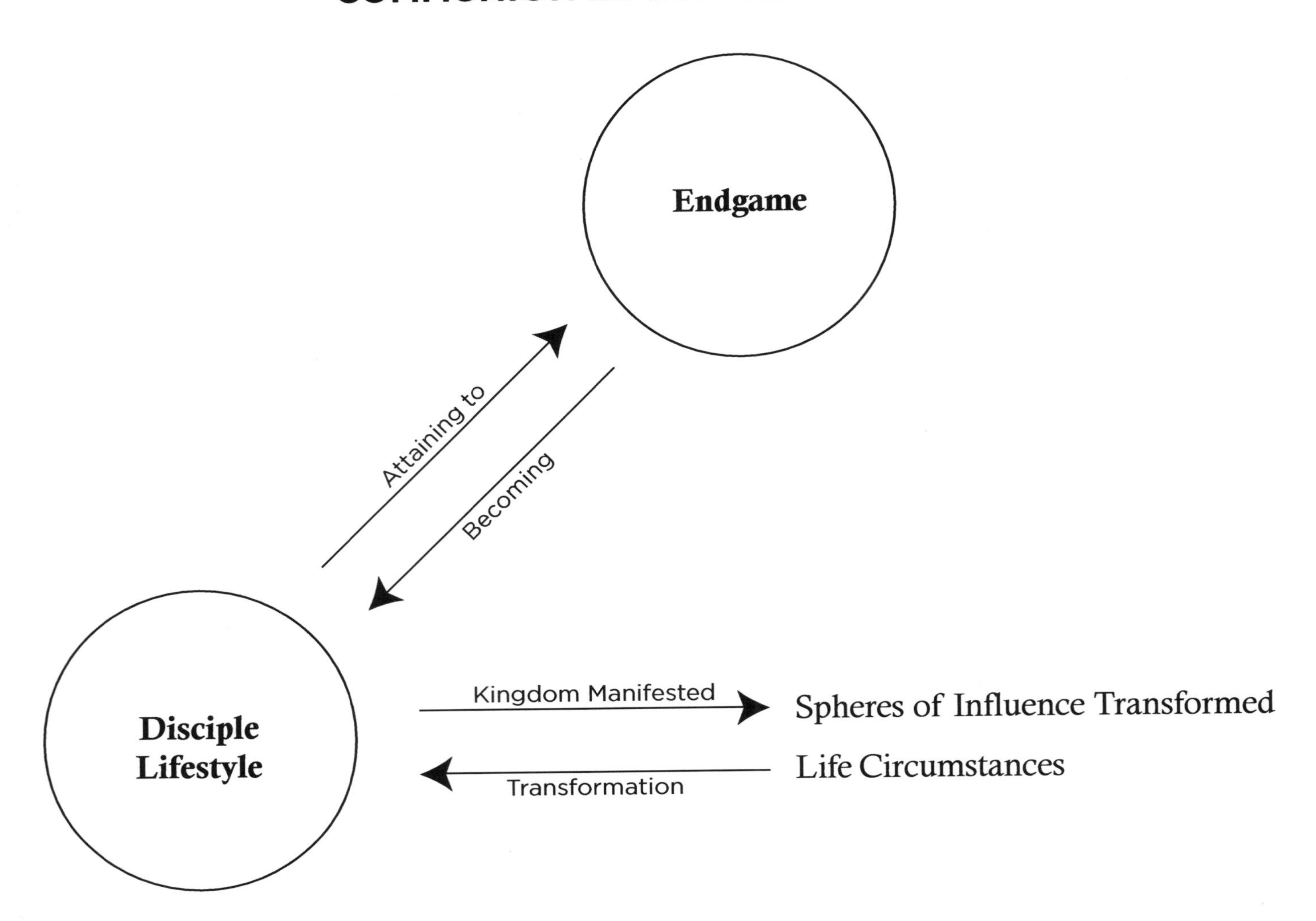

Disciple: A disciple is a person who habitually lives a self-sacrificial life abiding in the living person of Jesus Christ. Baptized with power, a disciple lives an experiential lifestyle in *__communion__ with the Holy Spirit, manifesting mighty acts of love, faith, gifts and signs.

**Communion* *is a person's participation with the presence of the Holy Spirit as He manifests the Spirit of Jesus Christ in their mortal flesh.*

The **Endgame** is to be joined and ***made perfect*** in the spiritual union of one with the Father, Son and Holy Spirit so the world will see through a disciple's life that the Father sent the Son and loves those in the world as He loves His Son. (John 17:20–23)

Kingdom: The Kingdom of God on earth as it is in heaven is the love of the Father manifested by the Son, Jesus Christ, through the royal and divine power of His Spirit and Word reigning in glory, honor and dominion in ALL creation.

Simplified: The manifestation of the fullness of the Spirit of Jesus Christ!

PUTTING IT ALL TOGETHER

The Communion Lifestyle diagram gives us a visual as to how all the different aspects of an authentic disciple's lifestyle come together. I will explain the diagram in a moment but let's first review what we've learned.

We've Learned:
What is the preeminence of Christ
What is an authentic disciple
What is a communion of the Holy Spirit lifestyle
What is the Endgame
What is the kingdom of God

Putting It All Together

As a disciple lives a lifestyle in communion with the Holy Spirit, the Holy Spirit uses life circumstances to transform them into the fullness of Jesus Christ. The Holy Spirit always has a disciple's life aimed towards the endgame. As a disciple becomes perfected in the spiritual union of one, the Holy Spirit increases and sustains more of the kingdom of God in a disciple, transforming spheres of their influence.

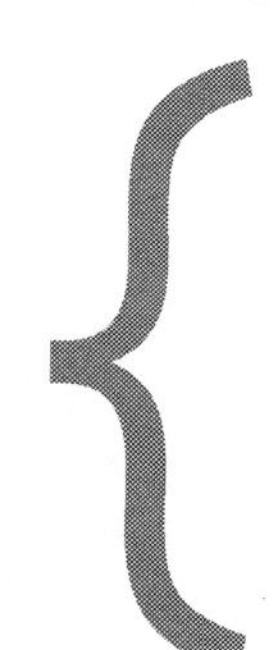

This is how authentic disciples in the workplace participate with the Holy Spirit Restoring the Preeminence of Jesus Christ in Business.

Date: ____________________

Meditate

Meditate on the diagram and the Putting It All Together statement. Your new lifestyle as an authentic disciple!

Journal

Journal what you saw, heard and pondered in your time of meditation.

____

____

____

____

____

____

____

____

Belief Statement

Document what you believe.

____

____

____

____

Prayer

"Ask anything according to Me and I will do it."

____

____

____

____

THE ULTIMATE UNFAIR COMPETITIVE ADVANTAGE!

THE ULTIMATE UNFAIR COMPETITIVE ADVANTAGE

"Jesus Christ is not an ROI"

I am a little better now but in years past I used to get so frustrated with business owners who thought they would automatically be blessed financially because they were Christians. One day alone in the car, my frustration peaked and I screamed as loud as I could, "Jesus Christ is not an ROI!" *(return on investment)*

"To me, who am less than the least of all the saints, this grace was given, that I should preach among the Gentiles the unsearchable riches of Christ, and to make all see what is the fellowship of the mystery, which from the beginning of the ages has been hidden in God who created all things through Jesus Christ; to the intent that now the manifold wisdom of God might be made known by the church to the principalities and powers in the heavenly places, according to the eternal purpose which He accomplished in Christ Jesus our Lord, in whom we have boldness and access with confidence through faith in Him."
(Ephesians 3:8–12, NKJV)

All authority in Heaven and earth belongs to Jesus Christ and only authentic disciples get to participate in manifesting the manifold wisdom of God. When the unseen presence of Jesus Christ is the reality in which you live, your participation will be as bold as a lion, knowing every principality and power in the heavenly places is inferior to your authority in Jesus Christ.

"The wicked flee when no one pursues, But the righteous are bold as a lion."
(Proverbs 28:1, NKJV)

Jesus knows all, sees all, past, present and future. He is all powerful, always present and hides nothing from those who participate with Him. If you need any more encouragement, consider this promise:

"Then once more you shall see the distinction between the righteous and the wicked, between one who serves God and one who does not serve him."
(Malachi 3:18, ESV)

The time is at hand when you will see a distinct difference between those who are with Jesus and those who are not. Pray for the mercy of God to be with those who will find themselves on the other side of Jesus' plumb line.

First seek the kingdom of God and His righteousness and all things will be added to you. (Mathew 6:33)

"Praise the Lord! Blessed is the man who fears the Lord, Who delights greatly in His commandments. His descendants will be mighty on earth; The generation of the upright will be blessed. Wealth and riches will be in his house, And his righteousness endures forever."
(Psalm 112:1–3, NKJV)

"Jesus Christ, a disciple's ultimate unfair competitive advantage!"

Date: ____________________

Meditate

As an authentic disciple every principality and power that opposes Jesus is inferior to His abiding presence with you. Meditate on living from this reality. Then start participating with the Holy Spirit pushing back the gates of hell. (Ephesians 3:10)

Journal

Journal what you saw, heard and pondered in your time of meditation.

Belief Statement

Document what you believe.

Prayer

"Ask anything according to Me and I will do it."

MAKING DISCIPLES

MAKING DISCIPLES

When I first started compiling these messages, I told a friend, "I think the Lord is having me write a book?" "He said, "Good, because if it's not in writing it's not replicable." When he said that it was as if the Holy Spirit physically pushed me. I realized as I caught myself that I just heard a word from the Lord. For the next three days I kept hearing over and over in my mind, if it's not in writing it's not replicable, if it's not in writing it's not replicable, if it's not in writing it's not replicable.

Be Fruitful & Multiply (replicate)

If you find yourself participating with the Holy Spirit in making disciples, I want to encourage you to use this material and the equipping style the Holy Spirit has given me.

But first, let me tell you the same thing the Holy Spirit told me prior to sending me out to CEOs. The Lord said, "the first thing you need to learn is how to come into agreement with me in what I'm doing in an individual's life." What I understood the Lord saying was, I could not minister from my experience or knowledge. Everything I do to live in participation with Him on an individual basis I was now going to have to do on behalf of others. My wife once said to me, "You spend more time praying and seeking the Lord for those you work with than they do for themselves." I said "Yeah you're right, It's my job."

Agreement

If you are not living in agreement with the Holy Spirit for your own life, you can be assured He's not going to bring you into agreement with what He's doing in another's. Seek the Lord to see that He has nothing against you. (Revelation 2:4) When you know you're living in agreement, (agreement, not perfection) then proceed in making disciples in communion with the Holy Spirit.

Equipping Style

As a spiritual shepherd I work side by side carrying disciple's burdens, prophetically mentoring them in how to live in partnership with the living presence of Jesus Christ through the lifestyle of communion with the Holy Spirit. I participate in agreement with the Holy Spirit, asking questions and offering experiential insights that challenge a disciple to seek answers from the Holy Spirit for themselves. This style facilitates a disciple to obtain divine illumination in ways that are unique to their perspective, resulting in a greater understanding, belief and activation in what the Holy Spirit is revealing to them.

Date: ____________________

Meditate
Making disciples in this manner is another level of self- sacrificial living. Meditate on counting the cost. (Luke 14:28) Then go start making authentic disciples. (Matthew 28:19-20)

Journal
Journal what you saw, heard and pondered in your time of meditation.

Belief Statement
Document what you believe.

Prayer
"Ask anything according to Me and I will do it."

A WORD TO
CEOs, PRESIDENTS & OWNERS

A WORD TO CEOs, PRESIDENTS & OWNERS

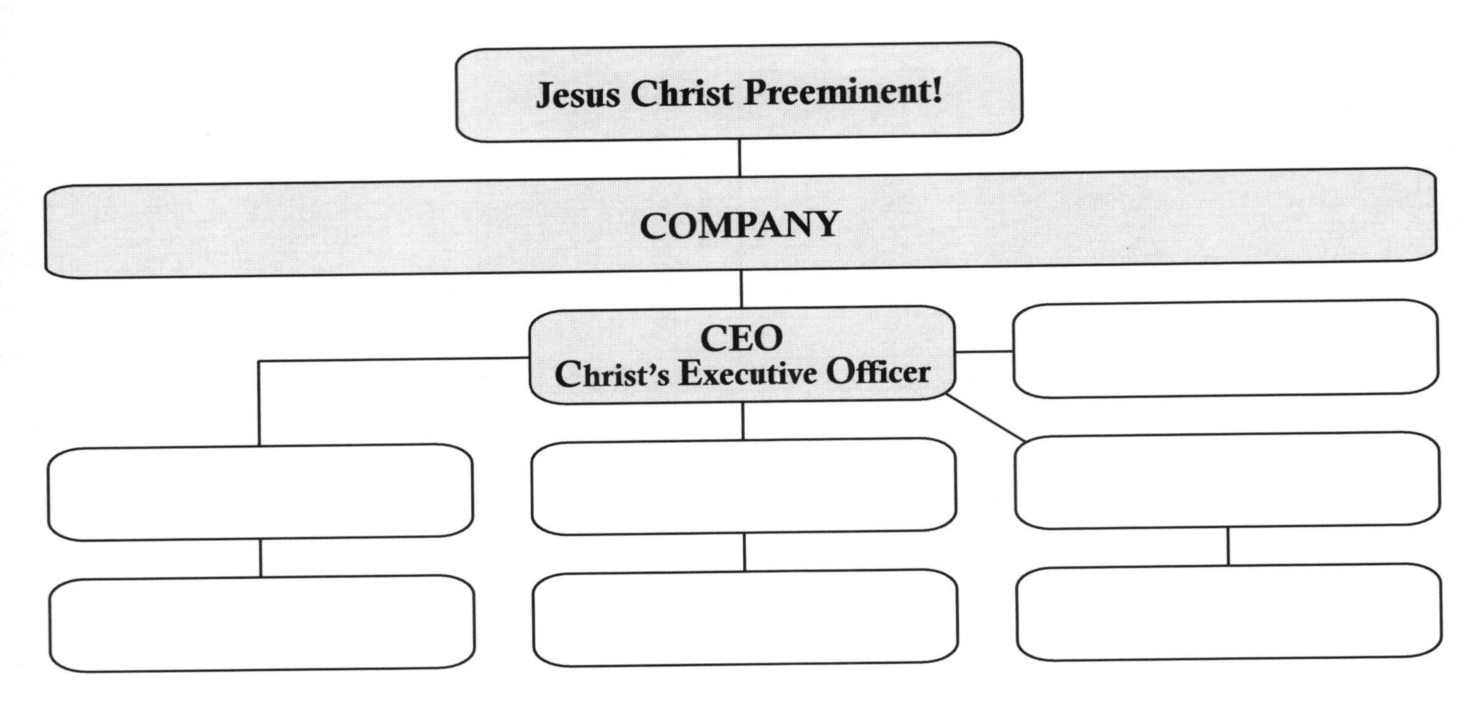

We have concluded that "all things" includes business and that authentic disciples live from a reality of the presence of Jesus Christ. Therefore a disciple participating with the primacy of Jesus Christ in business will never hold a greater position in Jesus' company then second-in-command. A bondservant is not greater than His master. It's these truths that inspired our term "Jesus Christ's CEOs" (Christ's Executive Officers). At Windows of Heaven the terms "Jesus Christ's CEO" and "authentic disciple" are synonymous.

Leader

If you were to study the word leader in the New Testament you would find it directs you to the word guide. Why is this important? Let's review what we have already learned.

"However, when He, the Spirit of truth, has come, He will guide you into all truth; for He will not speak on His own authority, but whatever He hears He will speak; and He will tell you things to come. He will glorify Me, for He will take of what is Mine and declare it to you."
(John 16:13–14, NKJV)

"But the Helper, the Holy Spirit, whom the Father will send in My name, He will teach you all things, and bring to your remembrance all things that I said to you."
(John 14:26, NKJV)

Guide is defined as "to lead the way." The Holy Spirit has been sent to the Church as the exclusive guide and teacher in all things pertaining to Jesus Christ.

Christ's Executive Officer

- As the Christ's Executive Officer, your first act of leadership is to honor and declare the primacy of Jesus Christ at all times. (Colossians 1:15-18)

- As the Christ's Executive Officer, your second act of leadership is to pattern for others how to do business heartily unto Jesus Christ in communion with the Holy Spirit. (Philippians 3:17, 1 Timothy 1:16, Titus 2:7 Colossians 3:23)

- As the Christ's Executive Officer, your third act of leadership is to equip others to do business heartily unto Jesus Christ in communion with the Holy Spirit. (Matthew 28:20, Ephesians 4:12)

In summary, guide means to direct the movement of others. The root meaning represents the conducting of one along the right path, implying: Leadership!

"Jesus said to him, "I am the way, the truth, and the life..."
(John 14:6, NKJV)

Team Jesus

I have seen the most amazing miracles happen in business when two or more believers were in agreement with how the Holy Spirit was leading in a business circumstance.

"Again I say to you that if two of you agree on earth concerning anything that they ask, it will be done for them by My Father in heaven."
(Matthew 18:19, NKJV)

"Most assuredly, I say to you, he who believes in Me, the works that I do he will do also; and greater works than these he will do, because I go to My Father."
(John 14:12, NKJV)

Trust me when I tell you, the team will be in awe of the miracles Jesus will do when His Body does business in agreement with the guidance of the Holy Spirit.

Date: ____________________

Meditate

For everyone to whom much is given, from him much will be required. (Luke 12:48) Meditate on the significance of what it means to be a Christ's Executive Officer.

Journal

Journal what you saw, heard and pondered in your time of meditation.

____

____

____

____

____

____

____

____

Belief Statement

Document what you believe.

____

____

____

____

Prayer

"Ask anything according to Me and I will do it."

____

____

____

____

THE HOLY TEMPLE OF THE SPIRIT OF GOD

THE HOLY TEMPLE BLUEPRINT

Ephesians 2:19-22

LOVE +	LOVE +	LOVE	= PERFECT LOVE
"You Shall **love** the Lord your God with all your heart, with all your soul, and with all your mind." **MATTHEW 22:38**	And the second is like it: "You shall **love** your neighbor as yourself." **MATTHEW 22:39**	The body knits together by joints supplying according to their workings. This causes growth to the body for the edifying of itself in **love**. **EPHESIANS 4:16**	Becoming perfect in one, bearing the **love** of the Lord to the world. **JOHN 17:23**
Faith experienced in communion with the Holy Spirit grows love for the Lord **EXPERIENCED**	One heart experienced in communion with the Holy Spirit grows love for our neighbors **EXPERIENCED**	Exercise Phase 1 and 2 in unison and the love of Jesus Christ joins and build up His Temple **LOVE + GROWTH =**	Jesus fills the Temple with the fullness of His glory **"LOVE"** **MANIFESTATION**
Wisdom exercised in communion with the Holy Spirit manifest faith **EXERCISED**	Oneness exercised in communion with the Holy Spirit develops one heart **EXERCISED**		
Seeking/Renewing practiced in communion with the Holy Spirit reveals wisdom **PRACTICED**	One Accord (mind & purpose) practiced in communion with the Holy Spirit develops oneness **PRACTICED**		
Phase 1 *Authentic Disciples*	**Phase 2** *Authentic Communities*	**Phase 3** *Territory Occupation*	**Phase 4** *Kingdom on Earth*

WINDOWS OF HEAVEN

THE HOLY TEMPLE OF THE SPIRIT OF GOD

When I was meditating on revival, the Lord gave me a vision of His glory and presence sustained in a very large geographical area. I was so excited to see His perpetual presence dwelling in the land, I asked if I could be part of it. He said, "Not only will you be part of it, but you will be on the front lines." The blueprint of the Holy Temple of the Spirit of God is the plan for making this vision a reality in any nation and their subcultures; *religion, family, government, arts/entertainment, media, business or education.*

"Now, therefore, you are no longer strangers and foreigners, but fellow citizens with the saints and members of the household of God, having been built on the foundation of the apostles and prophets, Jesus Christ Himself being the chief cornerstone, in whom the whole building, being fitted together, grows into a holy temple in the Lord, in whom you also are being built together for a dwelling place of God in the Spirit."
(Ephesians 2:19–22, NKJV)

Blueprint Explained

Phase 1, Make authentic disciples. Phase 2, Authentic disciples live in local communities. Phase 3, The Holy Spirit joins, knits and builds up local communities. Love plus growth equals territorial occupation. Phase 4, The fullness of the Kingdom is manifested and sustained through the Lord's Holy Temple on earth.

Did you notice? The Temple is entirely dependent on Phase 1. Authentic discipleship is the only form of communion with the presence of Jesus Christ. If theres no individual communion with Jesus, there can never be authentic community with the presence of Jesus Christ.

It is my belief through observation that the majority of the Body of Christ is not living as authentic disciples. As a result the Church has delayed it's right to participate in the dominion of the Kingdom of God on earth as it is in Heaven. I made this statement previously:

"The greatest hindrance in making disciples of the Church is that the churchgoing Christian already believes they are a disciple."

This isn't the first time people thought they were something they weren't. Review these other examples: Numbers 16, Matthew 7:21-23, Matthew 25:1-12, John 5:37-40. I trust you now remember a few other Bible stories.

We have many church leaders frustrated because they have proceeded with their people to Phase 2 and 3 without accomplishing Phase 1. Consequently many have become disappointed, tired and even quit their callings because they didn't see the Kingdom Phase 4 sustained in their people, communities and territories. I believe this blueprint outlines the change they've been praying for.

Engage

The act of engaging to live as an authentic disciple, not perfection, is the key here. Once a person makes a commitment with all their heart to live as an authentic disciple, they will immediately see glimpses of the Kingdom manifested in their life. As they habitually stay engaged in the lifestyle more of the fullness of the Kingdom will rule and reign their life.

Find another person living in covenant as an authentic disciple. You'll have yourself a community... and off you go!

Covenant

I long with all of my heart to see the Temple of God fill the earth. For this to happen the Church is going to have to live in covenant with Jesus as authentic disciples. I have made my covenant with Jesus. Will you join me?

My Covenant

Date: ____________________

____

____

____

____

____

____

____

____

CEOs, Presidents & Owners

If you are the CEO, President or Owner of any size company and have made the covenant to live as an authentic disciple, get connected with us at *windowsofheaven.com*. As a community of Jesus Christ's CEOs, we want to do everything we can to help one another make their places of business Holy Temples in the Lord, dwelling places of the Spirit of God.

I look forward to the Lord's timing in writing the next volume. Until then, let's offer ourselves wholeheartedly to live as authentic disciples.

May the grace of the Lord Jesus Christ, the love of God, and the communion of the Holy Spirit be with you all. Amen.

See You Soon,

Leray

23097932R00052

Made in the USA
San Bernardino, CA
05 August 2015